TAIPEI
THE CITY A

Core Pacific City
The 12-storey giant orb that fronts and Artech's mall is dubbed the Death Star. It is faced with glass bands and textured granite.
138 Bade Road, sec 4

Taipei Dome
Beset with controversy, the construction of the multi-use sports arena has been delayed by environmental and safety issues.
See p009

Sun Yat-sen Memorial Hall
Bauhaus meets the Qing Dynasty in Wang Da-hong's tribute to the father of modern China. The hourly changing of the guard is worth a look, as are its cultural diversions.
See p024

President International Tower
Japanese architect Kenzo Tange's 29-storey tower houses some decent restaurants, a few design boutiques and the Eslite flagship (see p061), comprising a bookstore and art gallery.
11 Songgao Road

City Hall
The footprint of this 1994 building resembles a pair of plus signs (double 10 in Chinese), marking Taiwan's national day on 10 October.
1 Shifu Road, T 2720 8889

Taipei 101
CY Lee's skyscraper was the highest in the world for most of the noughties. Peer over Taipei from the 89th-floor viewing deck.
See p013

Elephant Mountain
The city lacks green areas, so residents often head to the surrounding mountains to take advantage of the great hiking on offer.

INTRODUCTION
THE CHANGING FACE OF THE URBAN SCENE

Like most Asian cities, Taipei was built in a hurry; the majority of it was erected from the 1950s onwards as a low-rise mass of tile-covered concrete boxes, among the old structures in Chinese and Japanese styles. Yet this is a culture that prefers to find freedom within the safety of enclosures, and you'll be surprised by stunning interiors within the most commonplace shells. In the 1980s, the economy began to surge and the next decade saw the acceleration of urban renewal, of which Taipei 101 (see p013) is the milestone.

In recent years, an impressive finesse in hospitality design has been promulgated not only by big names like the W (see p016), but also home ventures such as Humble House (see p021). The classic Taiwanese aesthetic has a strong Japanese influence that remains from the colonial era in the first half of the 20th century. The island later fell under the spell of the West. Only now is it starting to come into its own. Taipei's World Design Capital 2016 title has inspired a public awakening thanks to a concerted effort to use architecture and design for the common good, and what is currently happening creatively here is more exciting than at any other time in history.

Of course, it has long had a thriving independent film and music scene, and a distinctive cuisine. This is a city of the night, and only when the neon starts to flicker does Taipei reveal its true allure. Its humid air fogs up with diffused light and, like a character in a Tsai Ming-liang film, you'll soon succumb to its quirky enchantment.

ESSENTIAL INFO
FACTS, FIGURES AND USEFUL ADDRESSES

TOURIST OFFICE
3 Beiping West Road
T 2312 3256
www.taipeitravel.net

TRANSPORT
Airport transfer to city centre
Buses run 24 hours and depart Taoyuan
Airport to Main Station every 15 minutes
(less frequently overnight). The journey
takes 55 minutes. The MRT will connect
the airport to the city centre in mid-2016
Car hire
Asia Rent A Car
T 2301 1153
Metro
www.metro.taipei
Taxis
Taiwan Taxi
T 4058 8888
Taxis can be hailed in the street or from
ranks at stations and in nightlife districts

EMERGENCY SERVICES
Emergencies
T 119
Pharmacy
Jeng Kang Pharmacy
22 Han Kou Street, sec 1
T 2371 2831
Police
T 2556 6007

INTERNATIONAL INSTITUTIONS
British Office Taipei
26th floor, 9-11 Songgao Road
T 8758 2088
ukintaiwan.fco.gov.uk
American Institute in Taiwan
7 Lane 134, Xinyi Road, sec 3
T 2162 2000
www.ait.org.tw

POSTAL SERVICES
Post office
118 Zhongxiao West Road, sec 1
T 2361 5752
Shipping
DHL
T 6603 8000
www.dhl.com.tw

BOOKS
The Soong Dynasty by Sterling Seagrave
(Harper Perennial)
**Taiwan Mod: A Journey Through
Taiwanese Design** by Marc Gerritsen and
Luuk van Heerde (Page One Publishing)

WEBSITES
Design
www.tdc.org.tw
Newspaper
www.taipeitimes.com

EVENTS
Taipei Arts Festival
eng.taipeifestival.org.tw
Taipei Biennial
www.taipeibiennial.org
Taiwan Designers' Week
www.designersweek.tw

COST OF LIVING
**Taxi from Taoyuan International
Airport to city centre**
TWD1,000
Cappuccino
TWD150
Packet of cigarettes
TWD70
Daily newspaper
TWD15
Bottle of champagne
TWD4,500

TAIPEI
Population
2.6 million
Currency
New Taiwan dollar
Telephone codes
Taiwan: 886
Taipei: 2
Local time
GMT +8
Flight time
London: 14 hrs 30 mins

AVERAGE TEMPERATURE / °C

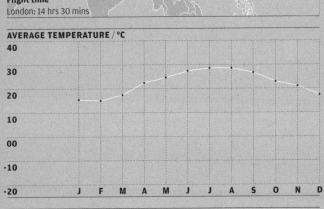

| | J | F | M | A | M | J | J | A | S | O | N | D |

AVERAGE RAINFALL / MM

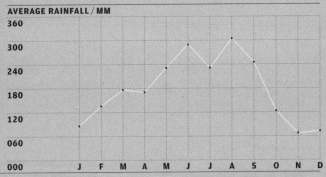

| | J | F | M | A | M | J | J | A | S | O | N | D |

NEIGHBOURHOODS

THE AREAS YOU NEED TO KNOW AND WHY

To help you navigate the city, we've chosen the most interesting districts (see below and the map inside the back cover) and colour-coded our featured venues, according to their location; those venues that are outside these areas are not coloured.

NORTH TAIPEI

Cross the Keelung River heading north and there is a lot of land left in Taipei, including most of the 1,120m Yangming Mountain. On its slopes you'll find private mansions and the hot-spring village of Beitou (see p025). Closer to downtown, Shilin is home to the city's best-known night market (see p080) and the Neihu area is filled with the sleek headquarters of Taiwan's top tech firms.

CENTRAL TAIPEI

The city's core, Zhongshan, is dominated by government offices and monuments, including Chiang Kai-shek Memorial Hall (see p014) and the Presidential Office (122 Zhongqing South Road, sec 1). Zhongshan North Road is lined with the flagships of luxury labels, and top hotels like Regent Taipei (see p017) and, around the corner, Palais de Chine (see p016). Nearby is Japan Town and the bustling Linsen North Road, which is as close to seedy as Taipei gets.

XINYI

This is the new Taipei, a mix of shopping malls and skyscrapers, many of which house bars or clubs on the lower levels; Barcode (see p054) is one of the best. Lorded over by Taipei 101 (see p013), the area was pre-planned as a growth zone, so it lacks the organic feel of the rest of the city, which is a softer, cosier jumble of residential and commercial. Xinyi is mostly brushed concrete, curtain-wall high-rises and ubiquitous advertising.

UNIVERSITY DISTRICT

The presence of National Taiwan University (see p076) gives this warren of boutiques, hip cafés and street food stalls a creative, bohemian atmosphere. But if the kids rule Shida and Gongguan, their professors head to Yongkang Street, which is as cultured as it is unpretentious, and not to be missed for its Taiwanese cuisine and tea houses, including Ye Tang (20-2, Lane 31).

EAST DISTRICT

This neighbourhood sets a high standard when it comes to local food, shopping and nightlife. Flanking Zhongxiao East Road is a department-store corridor (Dongqu), though the most interesting areas are the alleys and lanes that meander between the main boulevards. The zone to the north of Zhongxiao draws a young, cool crowd to its shops and plethora of bars, such as brewer Chuo Yin Shi (see p052). Daan Road is very good for fashion (see p080).

WANHUA

Taipei grew out of a settlement here along the Tamsui River, and several 18th-century temples still draw the throngs, and proudly display icons brought by early immigrants from China's Fujian Province. Surrounding these are many blocks of early 20th-century brick buildings dating back to the Japanese colonial era. Situated just to the south is supercharged Ximen — Taipei's answer to Shibuya. Its streets throb with school kids, fashion outlets and garish pop promos.

LANDMARKS
THE SHAPE OF THE CITY SKYLINE

In all but the labyrinthine old quarters, Taipei is a vast grid of wide, pedestrian-friendly avenues subdivided into lanes and alleyways. Viewed from the mountains ringing the city, two prominent towers serve as poles. In the west, <u>Shin Kong Life Tower</u> (66 Zhongxiao West Road) anchors the downtown area and sits across the street from the imperial-style <u>Main Station</u> (49 Zhongxiao West Road, T 2381 5226), opened in 1989. To the east is the blue-green <u>Taipei 101</u> (see p013), which presides over Xinyi's glassy high-rises and stores, the utilitarian 1986 <u>Taipei World Trade Center</u> (5 Xinyi Road, sec 5, T 2725 5200) and <u>Songshan Cultural and Creative Park</u> (133 Guangfu South Road, T 2765 1388), a development as ambitious as it is contentious. The old tobacco factory now houses the <u>Taiwan Design Museum</u> (T 2745 8199), and Toyo Ito's <u>Taipei New Horizon</u> (overleaf) has been built next door, but locals bemoan the loss of the leafy grounds to the oversized <u>Taipei Dome</u> and attendant mall.

The grand old boulevard Zhongshan Road runs north to south through the west of the city. At its southern end, the government district is signposted by the <u>Chiang Kai-shek Memorial Hall</u> (see p014), which overlooks Liberty Square. At its opposite extreme, the <u>Taipei Fine Arts Museum</u> (see p060) marks the end of downtown. The <u>Taipei Performing Arts Centre</u> (Chengde Road/Jihe Road), designed by OMA, will open across the Keelung River in 2016. *For full addresses, see Resources.*

Taipei New Horizon
The centrepiece of Songshan Cultural
and Creative Park, and a hub for WDC16,
houses shops, restaurants, a concert
venue, cinemas and a hotel (see p018).
Its curved, asymmetrically tiered form,
completed in 2013, nods to Le Corbusier
in the coloured accents of its concrete
grid facade, and its convex shape blocks
out noise from the busy freeway behind.
88 Yanchang Road, T 6622 6888

Hung Kuo Building

Local firm CY Lee & Partners has designed many of the most original skyscrapers on the island, including 101 (opposite). Its HQ is in the Hung Kuo Building, by far CY Lee's boldest postmodern structure, completed at the end of the 1980s. It's not hard to see how the inspiration for the trapezoidal massing came from the Egyptian sphinx and its angular headdress, and the Chinese character *sheng*, which means 'life'. Also look out for Chinese motifs in the granite, such as the wavy buttresses at the tops of the exterior pillars and interior columns. The architects were criticised for placing form before function here, and there are many unusual corners with unusable floor space. But in what is a mostly humdrum cityscape, we applaud the ambition. *167 Dunhua North Road, T 2514 7188, www.hungkuobuilding.com.tw*

Taipei 101

This 508m-tall postmodern pagoda, a dream made reality by CY Lee (opposite), held the title of the world's tallest building from 2004 to 2010. In low-lying Taipei, it stands out like Gulliver in a Lilliputian landscape: a glass-and-steel construction incorporating ancient Chinese motifs. The tiers feature *ruyi* (sceptre) designs, and mammoth 'lucky' coins appear at the split between the pagoda and the 34th-floor base. The super-tower is stabilised by three massive pendulums, the largest of which, at 660 tonnes, is visible from an upper-floor gallery. Though Taipei 101 has been described as disproportionate and ugly, no one complains on New Year's Eve when it's the scene of dazzling fireworks. There is an observatory on the 89th floor. *7 Xinyi Road, sec 5, T 8101 8899, www.taipei-101.com.tw*

Chiang Kai-shek Memorial Hall

A monument to the Chinese Nationalist leader Chiang Kai-shek, this building has been a controversial subject. In 2007, a pro-independence government changed its name to National Taiwan Democracy Memorial Hall, as they hated its neo-Qing dynasty connotations and the implication that Taiwan remains part of China. Just a year later, a pro-China president came to power and restored the original moniker.

Completed in 1980, the memorial was designed by Yang Cho-cheng – court architect to Chiang's exiled government. It looms over a gigantic plaza, which, like Tiananmen Square, was created as a dictator's parade ground. Despite the authoritarian overtones, the complex provides a lovely setting for a stroll.
21 Zhongshan South Road, T 2343 1100, www.cksmh.gov.tw

HOTELS

WHERE TO STAY AND WHICH ROOMS TO BOOK

Taipei experienced a tourism boom when direct flights between China and Taiwan resumed in 2009. One of the first to prepare for the influx of wealthy tourists – not only from the mainland but also further afield – was the Mandarin Oriental (158 Dunhua North Road, T 2715 6888), while the Regent Taipei (opposite) and Grand Hyatt (2 Songshou Road, T 2720 1234) unveiled sumptuous new looks. Xinyi is home to many highbrow names: Le Méridien (see p020), Humble House (see p021) and the W (10 Zhongxiao East Road, sec 5, T 8786 5168), which, with its sixth-floor lounge/bar/pool area, fits easily into the area's nightlife scene. For pomp and old-world glamour, The Grand Hotel (1 Zhongshan North Road, sec 4, T 2886 8888) is an imitation Qing palace just north of Taipei.

One of the pioneers of the boutique hotel scene was Éclat (370 Dunhua South Road, sec 1, T 2784 8888), a repository for real-estate mogul George Wang's huge art collection. Other smaller properties portray a patriotic spirit and, often, a nostalgic bent, with flavour coming from native culture and crafts in Amba's two hotels (see p022), while Home Hotel Daan (219-2 Fuxing South Road, sec 2, T 8773 8822) is 100 per cent made in Taiwan, from fit-out to dining. Local design star Ray Chen followed Palais de Chine (3 Chengde Road, sec 1, T 2181 9999) with equally hip Hotel Proverbs (56 Daan Road, sec 1, T 2711 1118); its steak house is an East District hotspot. *For full addresses and room rates, see Resources.*

Regent Taipei

An A-list destination since Michael Jackson stayed here in the early 1990s, the Regent set a new standard for the city's hotels in 2004 with its Tai Pan suites on the upper floors, due to the superior design details and service. Their continued popularity resulted in an expansion of the concept in 2011. Singapore-based Franklin Po decked out the original 80 rooms in a pared-back contemporary Chinese style, as seen in the Presidential Suite (above), which naturally comes with a round-the-clock butler. Even if you're not staying in one of these rooms, the Regent has an attractive, bustling atrium, where high-quality shops and top dining options draw locals as well as guests. Luxuriate at the Wellspring Spa (T 2523 8000), one of the city's best.
41 Zhongshan North Road, sec 2,
T 2523 8000, www.regenttaipei.com

Eslite Hotel
Set in the Toyo Ito-designed Taipei New Horizon (see p011), the latest addition to the Eslite juggernaut – the lifestyle and culture brand now has some 50 stores in Taiwan – is this design-forward hotel, which opened in 2015. An Eslite-branded bookshop, café, fashion boutique, theatre and cinema are also on site. The hotel's 104 rooms, with interiors by Hsuyuan Kuo Architects & Associates, feature works by local contemporary artists such as Benrei Huang, Su Wong-shen and Michael Lin, whose paintings use patterns appropriated from Taiwanese textiles. In the lounge, peruse more than 5,000 art, architecture and design titles from the comfort of a Minotti 'Prince' armchair or Mario Bellini sofa. The Library Suite (opposite) has as heavily stocked bookcase as you'd expect, and super views of Taipei 101 (see p013).
98 Yanchang Road, T 6626 2888,
www.eslitehotel.com

Le Méridien

This hotel is rather low-key for the vibrant Xinyi district. Singapore's LTW Designworks conceived the public areas as well as 160 rooms and suites, which feature a neutral palette of black, white and grey. There are close to 700 pieces of contemporary art spread throughout Le Méridien – Beijinger Li Hui's humongous steel resting-giraffe sculpture, *Be My Guest*, holds court in the lobby. The designer key cards are intended to be a keepsake, and provide free access to the Museum of Contemporary Art (see p057). Signature restaurant My Humble House serves authentic Cantonese cuisine in a thoroughly modern setting, and the more casual lounge is an ideal spot for an early evening cocktail. There is also an indoor lap pool and a slick fitness centre. *38 Songren Road, T 6622 8000, www.lemeridien-taipei.com*

Humble House

Another cultural oasis in the heart of Xinyi, Humble House, with interiors designed by HBA, sports muted tones and clean lines, which are the backdrop to an impressive art collection curated by Ellie Lai. Among the many highlights are *Bourrasque*, a commissioned 'floating' sculpture in the foyer by Londoner Paul Cocksedge, and, providing local colour, ink calligraphy by Tsai Char-wei and a video installation by Wu Chi-tsung. Of the 235 rooms, the Grand Premiers boast some of the best views. There's a sixth-floor sky garden, around which are set the bar/restaurant, serving Italian dishes. The Espace Beauté EB Spa (T 6631 8099) and outdoor rooftop pool (above; open April to November), a very urban setting for a dip, are also big draws. *18 Songgao Road, T 6631 8000, www.humblehousehotels.com*

Amba

Central Zhongshan is undergoing a major revival as its government buildings and monuments are joined by a raft of hip restaurants, design shops and this new hotspot. Taiwan's top environmental firm Bio-architecture Formosana (see p072), headed by Kuo Ying-chao, has cleverly transformed a 1970s office building into this stylish, 90-room hotel, which opened in 2015. The arcade-style entrance has been preserved, and Amba's southern facade is decorated with a pop art-style mural. The smart rooms – all with a fresh, soft palette – do what they say on the tin: the Large category (above) allows for the swinging of cats; the Corner category provides views of leafy Zhongshan North Road; and the Balcony category – well, you get the picture. There is another outpost in downtown Ximen (T 2375 5111).
57-1 Zhongshan North Road, sec 2,
T 2525 2828, www.amba-hotels.com

24 HOURS

SEE THE BEST OF THE CITY IN JUST ONE DAY

One of the joys of Taipei is its round-the-clock lifestyle, facilitated by the abundance of bicycles and cheap taxis that keep people moving from one area to another. Start with a traditional breakfast of *dan bing* (egg pancake) at a hawker food stall and set off on a cultural tour. The 1972 Sun Yat-sen Memorial Hall (505 Renai Road, sec 4, T 2758 8008), designed by Wang Da-hong and unmissable for its sweeping, orange-tiled roof, has a vast interior that contains galleries and a theatre, and is dedicated to the founder of the first Chinese republic in 1912. Close by, hip general store Good Cho's (54 Songqin Street, T 2758 2609) purveys excellent black sesame bagels, as well as locally made wares, from stationery to grooming products. For an overview of contemporary culture, MOCA (see p057) is an essential stop, as is the Taipei Fine Arts Museum (see p060). Nordic (22 Fuxing South Road, sec 1, T 2778 9667) is also worth visiting for its café/bar, and design store on the upper floors, which sells items by natives Calvin Lin and Liao Yi-hsien.

Taipei's culinary offerings are rich and diverse. Go with a group to Si Zhi Tang (18 Jinan Road, sec 3, T 8771 9191), where the light-touch cooking is based around fresh produce sourced from local markets. Sample the nightlife of the East District and Xinyi: the cocktails are best at R&D (see p053), or visit Marsalis (3rd floor, 90 Songren Road, T 8789 8166) for whisky and weekly jazz nights. *For full addresses, see Resources.*

09.00 Space Yoga

In the past few years, there's been a yoga boom in Taipei, with new centres popping up across the city. One of the best is Space, where the contemporary interior design enhances the feel of an urban sanctuary. The studios are clean-lined and airy, with plenty of natural light – surprisingly, this is a rarity among facilities in the city. The sleek downtown Anhe Road venue (above) also has a comfortable lounge with tiered cushions, which is a sociable chillout spot after class. For those in search of a full 24 hours of relaxation, stop off at Space's Tianmu branch (T 2877 2108), which has a peaceful garden, en route to North Taipei and the hot-spring district of Beitou. Stay overnight at Villa 32 (T 6611 8888), for its private springs and outdoor rock pools.
16th floor, 27 Anhe Road, sec 1,
T 2773 8108, www.withinspace.com

12.15 Huashan 1914 Creative Park

Often compared to Beijing's 798 art zone, also a former industrial complex, Huashan originated as a collective of galleries and studios, and is swiftly becoming a flashier and much more commercial showcase for Taipei's creative industries. Gone are the cutting-edge days (the mid-1990s) when an experimental theatre troupe was first to set up in this abandoned brewery, which was occupied by squatters at the time.

Today, the restored warehouses and pump rooms provide the backdrop for 1,000-capacity music venue Legacy, as well as film festivals and exhibitions. Tenants now include a yoga studio and some decent restaurants, such as VVG Thinking (T 2322 5573), a hip bistro and concept store set within a multi-level red-brick building. *1 Bade Road, sec 1, T 2358 1914, www.huashan1914.com*

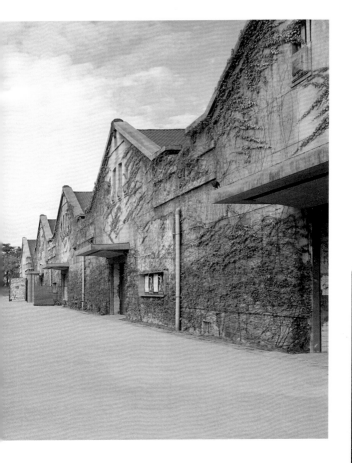

14.30 Cloud Gate Theater

Famous for a unique style that neatly melds Eastern and Western disciplines, including ballet, Chinese opera and Tai Chi, the Cloud Gate dance company has toured the world extensively under the direction of choreographer Lin Hwai-min since its formation in 1973. When its studio was destroyed by fire in 2008, the troupe procured generous private funding to build a far flashier theatre on government-leased land to the north of the city, atop a leafy hill overlooking the Tamsui River and Taiwan Strait. In 2005, the dancers performed a grand jeté into their new home, an organic, dark-green, almost-futuristic structure by Fieldoffice Architects. It is well worth the trip out here on the MRT to catch a matinee, best followed by a sundowner at the riverside La Villa Danshui (T 2626 8111).

36, Lane 6, Zhongzheng Road, sec 1, T 2629 8558, www.cloudgate.org.tw

18.00 Boven

In 2015, three enthusiasts launched this magazine library with around 20,000 titles stretching back two decades. There is a focus on design, fashion, lifestyle and the arts, and numerous rare and inaugural editions. Aiming to champion the printed word and bolster the survival chances of independents in the digital age, 300 new publications are added each month. The homey basement has two distinct spaces: one side has an office vibe, a communal table and old-school chairs; the other is a cosy living room (above), decked out with retro-style, black-leather armchairs and sofas by JusHouse. On arrival, you'll be offered slippers and a bespoke magazine trolley. Peace and quiet being paramount, only 20 readers are hosted at a time.
Basement, 18, Alley 5, Lane 107, Fuxing South Road, sec 1, T 2778 7526

20.30 Mountain and Sea House

Ho Yi-chia, who founded an organic co-op in Yilan County more than a decade ago, opened Mountain and Sea House in 2014 at the suggestion of her farmers. Indeed, vegetables often steal the show – bamboo shoots from Jiaoxi or okra from Ji'an, for example – in the simple, elegant dishes, which show off classic Taiwanese cuisine. The seafood is sourced from markets in Keelung and Penghu; try the deep-fried oysters and squid stuffed with three kinds of egg. The pork leg with Anka sauce is a speciality. Finish with oolong tea, served in Hsiao Fang ceramics. The restaurant is set in a traditional home, and interiors recall the grandeur of Japanese colonial rule. Staff uniforms are by designers Stephane Dou and Changlee Yugin (see p094).
16, Lane 11, Zhongshan North Road, sec 2, T 2511 6224

URBAN LIFE
CAFÉS, RESTAURANTS, BARS AND NIGHTCLUBS

In Taipei, a bowl of *pho* is as easy to find as Hunan or Cantonese cuisine. Chiang Kai-shek's retreat to Taiwan in 1949 brought more than one million migrants – and their culinary traditions – from every region of China. Factor in the Japanese occupation from 1895 to 1945, and later settlers from Vietnam and Thailand, as well as the thousands of Taiwanese who have now returned from living in the West, and you have a profuse mix of influences.

The city's renowned dumpling shop is Din Tai Fung (194 Xinyi Road, sec 2, T 2321 8928), where the *xiao long bao* (steamed soup dumplings) are heavenly. Fei Qian Wu (13-2, Lane 121, Zhongshan North Road, sec 1, T 2562 8701) serves some of the best homestyle *unadon* (eel bowl) outside Japan. To experience spicy Taiwanese hotpot, go to Shi Da Hua (2, Lane 209, An Ho Road, sec 2, T 2733 3589) or slick Host Shabu (see p038). Stop for tea – central to local culture – at South Street Delight (67 Dihua Street, sec 1, T 2552 1367). If you need a break from Asian fare, try Yannick Alléno's French restaurant STAY (4th floor, 45 Shifu Road, T 8101 8277).

Adjacent Xinyi and East District form the epicentre of Taipei's nightlife scene. When top DJs tour Asia, they play at club mecca Omni (see p054). If indie music is more your style, try The Wall (Basement, 200 Roosevelt Road, sec 4, T 2930 0162). Halo (8th floor, 12 Songshou Road, T 7737 9908) is a flashy cocktail spot. *For full addresses, see Resources.*

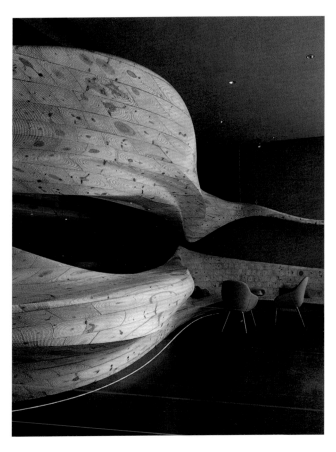

Raw

Taiwan-born chef André Chiang found success in Singapore with Restaurant André, and in Paris with Porte 12, before returning to Taipei to open Raw in 2014. The interior, by Singapore-based firm Weijenberg, features undulating wooden sculptural elements and custom-made furniture – cutlery and menus are hidden within drawers in the table. The cutting-edge design creates a fitting setting for Chiang's bistronomy-style cuisine, which gives an experimental bent to traditional dishes. The concise set menu highlights Raw's engagement with micro-seasonal local produce, and might include cobia fish with daikon, citrus and sago, and cod with charred cabbage and soubise. We suggest booking well in advance.

301 Le Qun 3rd Road, T 8501 5800, www.raw.com.tw

Shoun RyuGin

An outpost of the three-Michelin-starred Tokyo restaurant RyuGin, Shoun RyuGin opened in late 2014. The concise, seasonal menus are created by chef and founder Seiji Yamamoto (known for his *hamo* eel soup, for which he sourced a CT scan of the fish's anatomy in order to successfully negotiate the thousands of tiny bones in its body) and executed with aplomb by Ryohei Hieda, formally of Benu in San Francisco. Everything is driven by market availability; dishes might include clam soup with wood ear mushrooms and basil, *niawabi* (simmered abalone) or deep-fried sea urchin wrapped in nori. Ten Nen Sha, which also designed the Roppongi flagship, has conceived an elegant space serving just 36 at a time. Dinner only.
5th floor, 301 Le Qun 3rd Road, T 8501 5808, www.nihonryori-ryugin.com.tw

AGCT Apartment

An extension of the AGCT Group's lifestyle and clothing brand, established in 2009, the Apartment began life as a creative hub for local artists and designers. Open to the public since 2014, it's a relaxing spot hidden away on the third floor (it's best to call ahead, then ring the doorbell when you arrive) with floor-to-ceiling windows that overlook a tree-lined road. The café serves light and tasty Western lunches, such as croque madames and frittatas, and doubles as a small homewares outlet and fashion showroom. Wenzhou Street itself is a vibrant strip full of boutiques, eateries and bookshops. Check out the Good Design Institute (T 2362 0723), a café/concept store set in a private flat that hosts exhibitions and workshops.
3rd floor, 2-2, Lane 49, Wenzhou Street, T 2369 6659

Mitsui Cuisine

Sashimi aficionados should try the more exotic varieties, such as glass shrimp and sea urchin, at one of Mitsui's seven locations. The Neihu branch (T 2533 8802) is renowned for its high-powered political clientele; we prefer the East District venue (above) for its cavernous dining room, open kitchen and great set lunch menus. The prolific Ray Chen designed the interior, using a palette of dark tones, wood and white marble. The expansive central area is flanked by a long sushi bar and private booths, and a series of abstract sculptures perch on pedestals in various nooks. Make sure you are in your seat at 9.30pm for the closing ritual, when staff come out and bow to diners, and a curtain drops over the kitchen. *Basement, 108 Dunhua South Road, sec 1, T 2741 3394, www.mitsuitaipei.com.tw*

Host Shabu
Hotpot – a method of stewing food in a boiling broth at the table – is ubiquitous in Taipei. Popular ingredients at Host Shabu are the Kobe beef or lobster claw, with vegetables such as cabbage and yam. Rice is then added and the dish is boiled down to a porridge. The iron pots were designed by Sori Yanagi and the 'Wishbone' chairs by Carl Hansen & Søn.
28 Songren Road, T 2723 9222

Café Showroom

Set on laidback Fujin Street, this bright café, founded by Katherine Liu and Jamie Chung, is a lovely spot in which to discover the work of young local artists, such as Tzu Ting Wang, Wanyu Wang and Tien-Yu Lo. The homestyle lunch dishes include truffled egg toast, panini with fillings such as mushroom and spinach, and feta quiche. Seasonal smoothies and juices are also on offer, such as banana, grape and oolong.

There is a second branch (T 6636 5888) inside Eslite at Taipei New Horizon (see p010). Elsewhere on this hip stretch, keep an eye out for concept store Fujin Tree 355 (see p080), bijou Japanese homewares shop Beher (No 354; T 2765 2646) and ceramicist 3,co (No 377; T 8787 5271), for its tea sets and vases in natural glazes. *462 Fujin Street, T 2760 1155, www.cafeshowroom.com*

Wistaria Tea House

Named after the wisteria vines that are such a feature of its front courtyard, this 1920s Japanese-style wooden house was once a haven for political dissidents and avant-garde writers, including Pai Hsien-yung and Yin Haiguang. Today, the tea house continues to attract the illuminati. Its tranquil interiors, with tatami flooring and low carved tables, reflect the island's colonial heritage. Classic brews, such as traditional Chinese *tie guan yin* from the Fujian province and Taiwanese oolong, are served from terracotta pots into thimble cups, and accompanied by delicate savoury snacks and sweets made with sesame and red-bean paste. The art and ritual of the ceremony – from how to pour to when to refresh your leaves – is charming.

1, Lane 16, Xinsheng South Road, sec 3, T 2363 7375, www.wistariateahouse.com

Dozo Izakaya
Eschewing the cubby-hole design of a traditional izakaya, Kan Tai-lai left this acclaimed sashimi restaurant relatively open plan, although private booths ring the balcony, and there are cosier nooks below. The sweet shrimp and *maguro* (tuna) with cod roe and pickled turnip is one of the many highlights of the menu.
102 Guangfu South Road, T 2778 1135, www.dozoizakaya.co

Tua

Owner Chen Chao-wen made his mark on the city's culinary map with Si Zhi Tang (see p024). At Tua, which opened in 2014, he has also turned his hand to interior design, converting a two-storey house into a casual, polished restaurant, which features industrial elements alongside vintage Scandinavian furniture. Chen's contemporary Taiwanese cuisine uses produce sourced from local markets. He brings a refined and seemingly effortless touch to innovative dishes, including steamed wild fish with *kombu* seaweed, three-cup pork knuckle, foie gras with salted duck egg, and *kaoliang* (sorghum wine) marinated Taiwanese sausage. Do make yourself at home – *tua* is a Hokkien word for a spirited dinner with friends. *15-1, Lane 44, Siwei Road, T 2708 2082, www.tuaculture.com*

Non Zero

This East District eaterie does far more than wave a banner for organic food and low-impact living – it acts on these issues. Owner Chu Ping works closely with a group of local farmers, selling their vegetables from a stand near the restaurant's kitchen. For the interior design, Chen Chao-wen made great use of recycled materials. The herringbone marble floor was laid using stone-quarry scraps, and some of the walls were reclaimed from an old farmhouse. The facade is faced with tiles made of tree-fern wood, which is used for growing orchids; here it has sprouted a natural, mossy patina. The menu is seasonal, and includes stews, soups, pasta, curry and mountainous organic salads. Also try the excellent rack of lamb with herbs.

5, Alley 4, Lane 27, Renai Road, sec 4, T 2772 1630, www.nonzero.com.tw

Mume

Hong Kong-born chef Richie Lin's team at Mume, named after Taiwan's signature plum flower, has a collective experience that stretches from Noma in Copenhagen to Quay in Sydney and Per Se in New York. Lin's dishes make full use of the island's diverse produce – cherry radish, tuberose, ice plant and nasturtium, as well as local favourites such as duck heart and Chinese bacon – and are prepared using methods inspired by New Nordic Cuisine, including drying, pickling, fermenting and smoking. The minimal, industrial-style interior by Capella features grey tones, wood, metal, rope and low lighting – providing a stylish backdrop for the arty plating. A tasting menu is served for up to 12 in the private dining room. Mume is open for dinner only. *28 Siwei Road, T 2700 0901, www.mume.tw*

Kiosk

A casual 10-minute stroll from Huashan 1914 Creative Park (see p026), Kiosk is a modern European-style café run by Phil Hsu. Behind a midnight-blue facade, the spacious, uncomplicated interior of white walls, blondewood floors and black-stained furniture exudes a sense of calm. Secure a seat at one of the three tables that look out to the tree-lined street. Kiosk is famed for its *xiao bai* (flat white), but we prefer the cold-brewed shakerato, especially when accompanied by the lemon and olive oil cheesecake. Also on Xinsheng North Road is the laidback Debut Cafe (T 2541 7279), offering light bites and fantastic coffee – try the black sesame and green tea latte. It sells a selection of craft beers and house-roasted beans to take away. *40 Xinsheng North Road, sec 1, T 2542 8090*

Shi-Yang

In 1996, architect Lin Bin-hui opened
Shi-Yang restaurant on the slopes of
Yangming Mountain, before moving
it to the Taipei suburb of Xizhi City in
2009. Diners sit on tatami mats, or on
benches around long wooden tables.
Meals come in prix-fixe menus of 10
courses; the soups are phenomenal.
*7, Lane 350, Xiwan Road, sec 3,
T 2646 2266, www.shi-yang.com*

Chuo Yin Shi

A pioneer of the craft beer movement in Taipei, Chuo Yin Shi translates as The Tasting Room, and attracts both the hip crowd and the smart suits. A blackboard displays a rotating weekly list of 20 local and international labels, all of which are served on draught – the taps, pipes and gauges serve as the main design feature, amid an interior of recycled wood and exposed brick. Sample the Wabi-Sabi Japan Pale Ale, or a local tipple from the established 55th Street, or Chuo Yin Shi's fledgling house brand, Taihu. Soak up the alcohol with *luwei* – spicy braised snacks, such as duck wings. The venue doubles up as a display space for promising artists from across the island, including illustrator Jessica Lee, who created the bar's logo. *14, Alley 5, Lane 107, Fuxing South Road, sec 1, T 8773 9001, www.taihubrewing.com*

R&D Cocktail Lab

Identify the discreet doorway – scan the grey facade for the R&D symbol that roughly depicts the chemical structure of ethanol – and you will be rewarded with a bespoke cocktail, perhaps crafted from locally sourced ingredients such as lychee, mango or peach, and skilfully mixed by the self-styled 'Research and Developers'. The plush interior is a heady fusion of East meets West, with elements of a traditional British tavern cleverly melded with Oriental accents of red brick and Chinese herbal medicine cabinets. Snacks include ceviche with sweet potato crisps and street market-inspired slow-cooked pork belly with housemade pickled vegetables, peanuts and coriander. The best seats are close to the action, where you can watch the bartenders at play.
178 Yanji Street, T 2778 9008, www.r-d.tw

INSIDER'S GUIDE

LESLIE SUN, BOUTIQUE/GALLERY OWNER

Following a 15-year stint in Los Angeles, Leslie Sun returned to her native Taipei and opened concept store Sunset (see p092) in the Daan district, where she now spends most of her time. On a day off she might cycle to Dajia Riverside Park in the north – 'it's such a peaceful place' – or spend the afternoon browsing contemporary art at MoNTUE (134 Heping East Road, sec 2, T 2732 1104). In the evening, she shares a hotpot with friends at Orange Shabu Shabu (Basement, 135 Daan Road, sec 1, T 2776 1658), popular with die-hard foodies: 'Its congee is heaven.' Afterwards, she satisfies her sweet tooth with a helping of carrot cake from Kiosk (see p048). When friends are visiting, she likes to show them around Dihua Street – 'where old and new Taipei mix' – before securing the best table at speakeasy-style Ounce (40, Lane 63, Dun Hua South Road, sec 2, T 2708 6885), which is tucked behind a hidden door.

Sun considers the nightlife here to be the best in Asia, and evenings will often start with seafood *donburi* at no-reservations Man Zhe Die (17, Alley 9, Lane 346, Bade Road, sec 2), followed by people-watching at The Den at Barcode (5th floor, 22 Songshou Road, T 2725 3520) and early hours spent at megaclub Omni (5th floor, 201 Zhongxiao East Road, sec 4, T 8380 3388). If you've still got energy to burn, Sun suggests one of the 24-hour KTV karaoke spots dotted across town. 'They actually serve very good food.'
For full addresses, see Resources.

ART AND DESIGN

GALLERIES, STUDIOS AND PUBLIC SPACES

Taiwan's art scene is often overshadowed by that of its neighbours China and Japan, but it does have plenty to shout about. Its public institutions act as an incubator, and MOCA (opposite) and the Taipei Fine Arts Museum (see p060) have taken a leading role in promoting homegrown talent. The Neihu area has grown into a hothouse, home to authoritative enterprises such as Liang Gallery (see p068), Tina Keng (15, Lane 548, Ruiguang Road, T 2659 0798) and its upstart TKG Plus (T 2659 0698), which joined forces with neighbouring galleries to form the Taipei Art District in 2014. The annual Art Taipei was founded back in 1992, and Photo Taipei and Young Art Taipei (see p069) were established at the end of the noughties, contributing to what is now a strong foundation.

Taipei is proud to have been designated World Design Capital 2016, and although it was the only city to put in a bid, it shows an official recognition of the value of aesthetics, and gives hope that traditional craftsmanship, such as that found at Ri Xing (see p070), might remain viable. There is still a certain Japanese and Scandi influence in the contemporary field, but local firms such as Viichen (see p063) are forging a new identity. In another encouraging sign, talented designers including Yenwen Tseng and Kenyon Yeh (see p063), who were educated abroad, are these days returning home to establish studios and bolster a flourishing movement.
For full addresses, see Resources.

MOCA

The esteemed Museum of Contemporary Art (MOCA) is steeped in history. It was built as a school under Japanese rule in 1919; after the war it was converted into City Hall before becoming Taiwan's first institution dedicated to modern art in 2001. Showcasing mainly local artists, such as new-media star Yao Chung-han ('Light On-Site'; above), it also exhibits retrospectives of prominent Asian names, for example China's Xiang Jing and Japan's Reiko Nireki. Under director Shih Jui-jen, MOCA's activities have become increasingly international – it hosted a solo show of Taiwanese painter/sculptor Yang Maolin at the 2009 Venice Biennale. It also promotes a rich public art programme, including the installation of works at metro stations. *39 Changan West Road, T 2552 3721, www.mocataipei.org.tw*

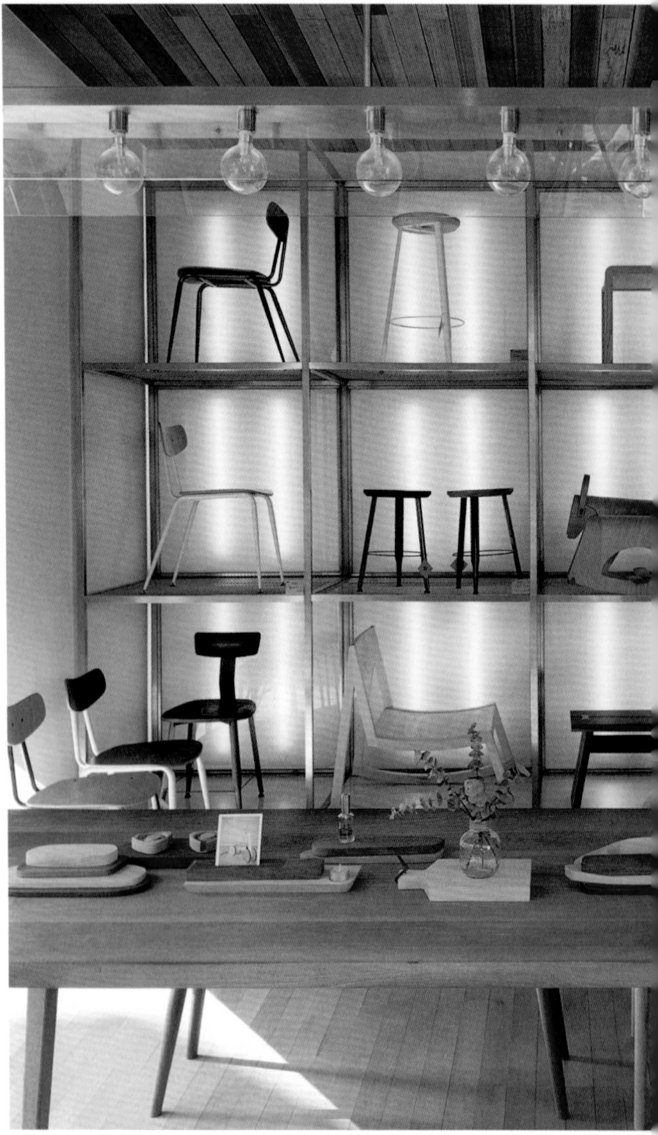

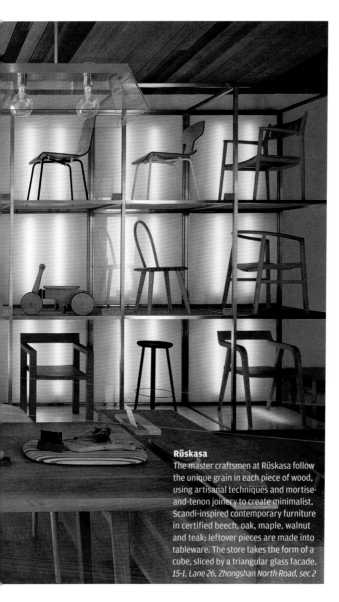

Rüskasa

The master craftsmen at Rüskasa follow the unique grain in each piece of wood, using artisanal techniques and mortise-and-tenon joinery to create minimalist, Scandi-inspired contemporary furniture in certified beech, oak, maple, walnut and teak; leftover pieces are made into tableware. The store takes the form of a cube, sliced by a triangular glass facade.
15-1, Lane 26, Zhongshan North Road, sec 2

Taipei Fine Arts Museum
Architect Kao Er-pan's minimalist design for the 1983 Fine Arts Museum, the host venue for the Taipei Biennial, consists of a series of white rectangular tubes stacked three storeys tall. Seen from above, they form the Chinese character for 'fountain', conveying the idea of a cultural wellspring. Taiwan's creative community developed a love-hate relationship with the structure, criticising its austere form and exhibition spaces. In 2010, the institution took heed of its critics and added a more human-scaled south entrance, designed by Chien Architects and Associates. Comprising a cantilevered glass corridor, and featuring crisscrossing angular beams, it facilitates access to the lovely park at the museum's rear. There is a good bookshop here too.
181 Zhongshan North Road, sec 3,
T 2595 7656, www.tfam.museum

Eslite Gallery

Retail giant Eslite (see p018) opened an art gallery at the same time as launching its debut bookstore in 1989; its founder, Robert Wu, was one of just a few at the time promoting contemporary Chinese and Taiwanese artists in Taipei. In 2009, the gallery, a three-hall space by designer Ray Chen, moved to the brand's flagship store in the Xinyi district. The collection features many notable luminaries from across mainland China, Hong Kong and Taiwan, including Xu Bing, Michael Lin, Liu Xiaodong, Cai Guo-qiang and native Lai Chih-sheng, who showed *Beyond Untitled* (above) in 2015. A committed youth programme ensures that fresh talent is given exposure alongside more established names. Closed Mondays.
5th floor, 11 Songgao Road, T 8789 3388, www.eslitegallery.com

Han Gallery

Established in 2011 by Han De-chang, Han represents a first-rate group of emerging local design talent, led by Gijs Bakker, the Dutch co-founder of Droog. Its focus is to sustain cultural values by presenting them in a contemporary framework. Tong Ho's 'Mirror Lattice' (above), for example, riffs on windowpane patterns from traditional Chinese architecture, cast in reflective pieces of stainless steel. Other significant works are Liao Po-ching's 'Calligraphy Screen', fashioned from driftwood found in the aftermath of Typhoon Morakot, as well as Pili Wu's 'Plastic Classic' chair and line of delicate tableware, whose ribbed porcelain alludes to the disposable plastic utensils used in the city's roadside cafés. Some items are available at Eslite in Xinyi (see p061); all can be purchased online. *www.han-gallery.com*

Viichen Design

Taiwanese design has traditionally been centred on clever gadgets and electronics, but fresh creatives are making waves with sophisticated takes on both furniture and product. Kenyon Yeh is one to watch due to his minimal, highly polished style. His pastel 'Yeh Side Table' was manufactured by Danish brand Menu; in Taipei, discover his work at Loft 29 (T 2773 0129). Another inspiring local studio is Viichen Design, which favours natural materials – founder Vii Chen launched with a line of textured porcelain cups. Her 'Interlaced' screen and lamp (above) is delightfully geometric and contemporary, yet the metal screens set before a bulb mimic an obscured view of the moon, as seen through the window of an old house. There are select pieces at Huashan 1914 Creative Park (see p026). *www.viichendesign.com*

World Trade Center Square
Toyo Ito's landscape design offers brief
green-space respite in the heart of Taipei,
its sinuous travertine pathways spiralling
across an expansive lawn – it's a popular
lunch spot for office workers. From the
Taipei 101 (see p013) observatory, a bird's-
eye view reveals its flower-like form. It
looks particularly lovely at night, when lit
up by LEDs that fringe the promenade.
5 Xinyi Road, sec 5

MRT subway art

Just one of more than 50 artworks that decorate the MRT network, *Fast or Slow* (above) by the Japanese artist Koichiro Miura was installed in the tunnel between stations at Nangang Exhibition Center in 2010. LEDs in the anodised aluminium panels are controlled by motion sensors, set off by footfall so that the lights 'follow' pedestrians – a background of spirals on one wall represents water, and stylised trees feature opposite. Situated at such a busy interchange, it is intended to provide a calming presence. Also worth checking out is Philadelphia sculptor Ray King's *Dancing Feathers Ascending in the Wind*, located in the entrance to Luzhou station, a suspended kinetic artwork of stainless steel and coloured glass that refracts sunlight from the domed ceiling overhead onto the walls and black granite floor.

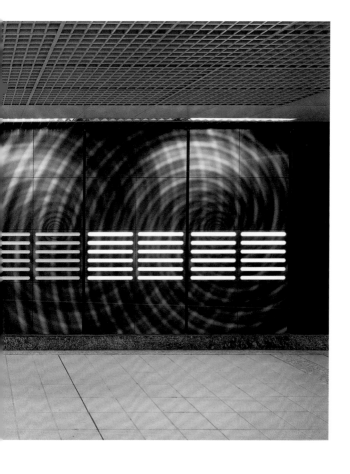

Liang Gallery

This is the authority on modern Taiwanese art. Its major exhibitions have included 'Tribute to the Masters' at Zhongshan Hall in 2015, which commemorated the 120th anniversary of the birth of Huang Tu-shui, and also featured the work of 11 other eminent sculptors, such as Chiu Yunn and Paul Tien-shen. In 2012, 'The Origin of Taiwan Art' (above) showed the paintings of Chen Cheng-po, a highly influential figure in postwar Taiwan. Founded by Yu Yen-liang in 1993, the three-storey space, with double-height ceilings and skylights, is situated in the emerging arts district of Neihu. Working with local foundations and international institutions, Yu is not only educating the nation, but also achieving record-breaking prices in the market.
366 Ruiguang Road, T 2797 1100, www.lianggallery.com

Galerie Grand Siècle

As a diplomat, Chang Hsueh-kung spent six years in Paris, where he was inspired by the city's diversity of galleries, and founded Grand Siècle on his return home in 1999. The focus has always been on Taiwanese talent, such as the Kaohsiung-born painter Liu Yi-lan ('An Affectionate Portrait of the Island'; above), and it has become renowned for exhibitions in new media, video, sound and light. The roster features some of the biggest names in the scene, including Chang Teng-yuan, who specialises in illustration and animation, and installation artist Ding Chien-chung; pieces are now being acquired by national museums. Chang also co-founded Photo Taipei and Young Art Taipei in 2009, which attracted more than 40 local galleries.
17, Alley 51, Lane 12, Bade Road, sec 3,
T 2578 5630, www.changsgallery.com.tw

Ri Xing Type Foundry

The centuries-old craft of letterpress printing lives on here, where Zhang Jie-guan has transformed the business his father started in 1969 into a living museum. Since 2013, it has been the last lead foundry in Taiwan; and has two million pieces of type in the three major fonts in seven sizes. It is the only place in the world to still sell complete sets of traditional Chinese script, which comprises 10,000 characters; following Mao Zedong's revolution, the pictographs used for millennia were simplified into new symbols on the mainland. Some of the fonts, such as *Song*, are more than 1,000 years old, while newer products include a stamp of the double happiness character. Zhang offers daily tours. *13, Lane 97, Taiyuan Road, T 2556 4626, www.letterpress.org.tw*

ARCHITOUR

A GUIDE TO TAIPEI'S ICONIC BUILDINGS

Taipei was settled in the early 18th century along the banks of the Danshui, and over time the city spread east. Near the river, the 1738 Lungshan Temple (211 Guangzhou Street), despite having been repeatedly rebuilt following fires and damage in WWII, remains spectacular; it has the southern Chinese influence typical of classic Taiwanese architecture. From here, head to the centre through the arcaded streets laid out in the early 20th century by the Japanese. When Chiang Kai-shek arrived in 1949, he named them after cities in China, as if Taipei were a scale model of the mainland.

In the 1960s, Wang Da-hong, who studied under Walter Gropius alongside Philip Johnson and IM Pei, introduced modernism to the island – Sun Yat-sen Memorial Hall (see p024) melds Bauhaus and Chinese forms. Not far away, the Hung Kuo Building (see p012) embodies 1980s postmodernism. By the 1990s, Kris Yao's practice Artech, which he founded in 1985, had designed a raft of high-tech towers to match Taiwan's IT boom, many along Dunhua Road; his 1999 CEC Building (100 Minsheng East Road) has an exoskeleton of concrete pillars and X-shaped girders. Some of the most exciting projects are now on uni campuses (see p079) and in the suburbs. In Beitou, Bio-architecture Formosana's Taipei Public Library (251 Guangming Road) evokes Japanese-era bungalows. Constructed from sustainable timber, its roof is clad with grass and solar panels. *For full addresses, see Resources.*

Zhonghe Sports Center

The unconventional volume of this sports centre, at first glance seemingly randomly plonked in the corner of a park in the outer suburbs, is an interesting example of the current mood of innovation that permeates Taiwanese architecture. Rather than simply build an identikit box, and in response to budget and environmental considerations, local firm Q-Lab stacked various levels of recreational facilities into an elongated 38m-high faceted hexagon and clad it in a reflective aluminium skin, bookending the edifice with huge glazed walls. An adjacent grass-roofed sunken arena reduces visual impact and keeps temperatures low. Q-Lab stated that the functionality of the easily assembled main body determined its form, but its designers likely had a lot of fun too. *350-1 Jinhe Road, T 2242 9222, www.zhsports.com.tw*

Water-Moon Dharma Center

Thanks to tall perimeter walls keeping out city hubbub on one side, and the river and mountains offering serenity on the other, this is a supremely spiritual, tranquil site. The religious complex was designed by one of the fathers of contemporary Taiwanese architecture, Kris Yao, using concrete and teak, as well as carefully placed natural elements (opposite), which adhere to Zen principles. Set in a lotus pond, the Grand Hall (above) comprises a wooden box on a glazed base that appears to hover below a flat roof supported by 22 majestic columns. Immense timber panels throughout are carved with sutras in Chinese script that not only provide inspiration, but also allow natural light inside meditation spaces and corridors. There are daily guided tours.
89, Lane 65, Daye Road, T 2893 3161, icd.ddm.org.tw

College of Social Sciences, NTU
The Taiwanese have been keeping Toyo
Ito occupied (see p010), and with good
reason. His 2013 university faculty is a
mammoth block that would have been
claustrophobic were it not for irregular
openings and a central void, which lends
it a certain lightness. As does the lotus-
leaf design of the plaza and library roof,
which 'blooms' from 88 concrete roots.
1 Roosevelt Road, www.coss.ntu.edu.tw

Taoyuan Airport Terminal 1

Taiwan's international airport, designed in 1979 by engineer Tung-yen Lin, was only intended to process some five million passengers annually – 30 years on, the footfall had tripled. In 2013, Japanese firm Norihiko Dan and Associates created this ingeniously simple, eco-friendly solution. The terminal's existing catenary roof was extended on both sides so that it draped to the ground, and then boxed in at each end. Not only did this create extra space without the need to construct additional floors, but it is also the airport's most striking element, the dramatic swoop and interplay of light and shadow providing a delightful welcome. From the exterior, the rows of louvred aluminium tiles are in keeping with the East Asian vernacular.
9 Hangzhan South Road, T 3273 3728, www.taoyuan-airport.com

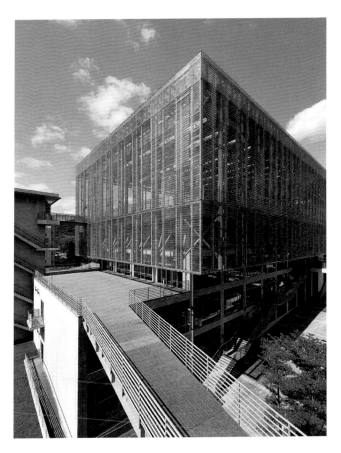

Shih Chien University Gym and Library
Taipei's educational institutions are at the forefront of the architectural avant-garde. In the city centre, check out NTUT's Green Gate (1 Zhongxiao East Road), a towering steel 'tree' covered in foliage and irrigated by solar power. Nature also inspired parts of the NTU's College of Social Sciences (see p076). Out past the city airport in Dazhi, Shih Chien University boasts another two triumphs for Kris Yao – the 2005 College of Design, and the 2009 Gym (above) and Library, two masculine silver-grey blocks shrouded in steel mesh that face off across a below-ground conference centre. Angular staircases, bridges and walkways provide circulation. The library is shaded by vertical louvres and has a cut-out plaza at its heart, while the upper part of the gym is almost transparent, especially when lit up at night. *70 Dazhi Street, www.lib.usc.edu.tw*

SHOPS

THE BEST RETAIL THERAPY AND WHAT TO BUY

One Taipei shopping trip you should not miss is a visit to a night market, where stalls are piled high with fashion, gadgets and food. Open from 6pm until after midnight, Shilin (60 Jihe Road, T 2882 0340) is the biggest; Snake Alley (Huaxi Street) the most touristy; and Tonghua Street the most diverse – try an ice-cream *run bing*.

For a more genteel experience, head to one of the two high-end shopping areas. Global luxury brands locate their flagship stores along Zhongshan North Road, where you'll also find SPOT Film House (No 18, sec 2, T 2511 7786) – an arthouse cinema with a tiny design shop and café set within the former American ambassador's residence. The other upmarket retail strip is Daan Road; seek out native designers Jamei Chen (No 132, sec 1, T 8773 0920) and Isabelle Wen (No 118, sec 1, T 2771 9021). Chifeng Street and its surrounds is now a hotspot for hip lifestyle stores, exemplified by Everyday Ware & Co and Xiaoqi (see p085). Further east, leafy Fujin Street makes for ideal strolling, with homey cafés (see p040) and small, chic concept stores – Fujin Tree 355 (No 355, T 2765 2705) sells a selection of beautiful Japanese homewares.

Buy tea at 120-year-old roaster Wang's (26, Lane 64, Chongqing North Road, sec 2, T 2555 9164) or Wang De Chuan (95 Zhongshan North Road, sec 1, T 2561 8738), which was founded in 1862. For superior packaging, source your oolong from PROT (see p091). *For full addresses, see Resources.*

22 Design Studio

Husband and wife team Sean Yu and Yiting Cheng launched their studio in 2005 (the name references their ages at the time), and were cited as designers to watch by Wallpaper* back in 2008 for their terrazzo effect 'Bare Ring'. Inspired by the city's built environment, the pair chose concrete as their primary material, using it to craft jewellery, stationery and timepieces. The solid '4th Dimension Table Clock' (above), TWD3,200, is tilted at 60 degrees for ease of view, and has an Escher-like stepped face; cantilevered brass hands complete the industrial look. There is also a wristwatch version, which is finished with a hand-stitched leather band in tan, peach or black. Select items can be found at homewares store Nest (T 6639 9948) in the Xinyi district. *T 2395 1970, www.22designstudio.net*

Invincible

A watershed store for slick menswear in Taipei when it opened in 2007, Invincible remains one of just a handful of retailers in Taiwan where you can source high-end Japanese streetwear labels such as Visvim, Sophnet and Uniform Experiment. Its East outpost (above) – there is another shop in the Ximen area – reopened in 2015, with a highly polished refurbishment: dove-grey interiors feature brass and Perspex shelving, a plywood counter and bronze racks. Invincible has global prestige for its limited-edition sneakers, collaborating with the likes of Reebok, New Balance, Adidas and Losers. It also stocks a line of Carhart WIP accessories, and a range of scents from Tokyo-based RetaW; we liked the travel-friendly Fragrance Tablets.

3, Alley 35, Lane 181, Zhongxiao East Road, sec 4, T 8771 9958, www.invincible.com.tw

Club Designer

A mecca for fans of European style, Club Designer was established in 1981 by Lilian Kao, who introduced fresh (then later renowned) fashion names to Taiwan. The five-storey shop is home to more than 90 brands, encompassing both international labels and up-and-coming talent, such as Ellery and Mansur Gavriel, which are showcased among Kao's collection of auction-house-quality vintage furniture.

There's a café furnished with Fornasetti and Jean-Charles Moreux, plus a selection of books, situated on the top floor (above). The basement houses the younger, funkier CLUB 1981, which is run by Kao's daughter Yi Chen and offers an edgier selection, including Mastermind from Japan, Bella Freud from London and MSGM from Italy. *133 Daan Road, sec 1, T 2777 4288, www.clubdesigner.com.tw*

Everyday Ware & Co

Housed inside an unassuming storefront, Everyday Ware & Co (above and overleaf) sells a mix of new and vintage items, with an emphasis on simple, well-crafted tools and objects for the house. We were taken by the Puebco canvas pot-holders, Amabro ceramics, Matsunoya aluminium plates and the porcelain by Taiwanese illustrator Zishi. There are a number of similar stores in the area. Xiaoqi (T 2555 6969) added some panache to Chifeng Street, which was known for its traditional metal workshops, in 2012. Stock up on Japanese homewares, such as Osamu Saruyama-designed coffee sets, and Hakuji Kodakatie pottery. Also on the same stretch, seek out its café, Xiaoqi Syokudou (T 2559 6851), and the plum-wine store Xiaoqi Umeshya (T 2559 6852). *25, Lane 20, Zhongshan North Road, sec 2, T 2523 7224, www.everydaywareco.com*

Lucky Brass Tag

Artifacts

The flagship of concept store Artifacts, whose manifesto is to bring online trends straight to the shop floor, was designed by Michelle Wei and Cheng Chia Hao in 2011. Located in the vibrant Daan retail district, it had to stand out, and that it does, thanks to a glass cube that protrudes from the facade showing eye-catching installations. Displayed within a monochrome interior are fashion and accessories by more than 50 global brands, in addition to grown-up toys, technology and lifestyle items, from Francis Kurkdjian perfume to headphones by Master & Dynamic and shoulder bags by M2Malletier. A further six (and counting) branches are dotted across town, each of them with slick schemes by local studios, such as Straight Square and MW Design.
23, Lane 177, Dunhua South Road, sec 1, T 2731 0682, www.artifactsstore.com

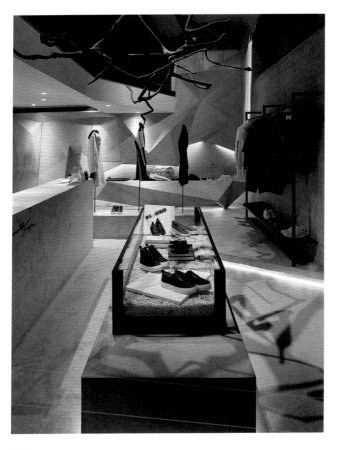

Ne Sense

This concept store was established by local brothers Steve, Michael and Richard Hsieh as a showcase for high-quality, functional menswear. Very well curated, Ne Sense offers emerging Asian labels, including DressedUndressed from Japan, and more established international brands, such as Stampd and Fear of God; we liked Ne Sense's own accesories line and took home a natty wool sports cap.

Interior design firm Yun-Yih used the five Chinese elements — earth, water, metal, wood and fire — as inspiration for the fit-out, which is realised through details including concrete flooring and fixtures, and a tree-branch sculpture suspended from the ceiling. A minimal palette lends the space a museum-like quality.
*1st floor, 52 Keelung Road, sec 2,
T 2729 1219, www.ne-sense.com*

小茶栽堂

Zenique

Founded in 2006, Zenique was a pioneer in the production of 100 per cent organic tea, which it sources from all across the island. There's a range of black and green varieties, and a delightful semi-fermented oolong. The brand champions 'respect for nature in pursuit of a pure lifestyle', and its minimal packaging won a Design Award in Japan. Similarly zen, thanks to its neat typography, living walls, and classical music, are the store (above) and a three-storey café on Yongkang Street (T 2395 1558), which is styled as if it were a fashion boutique, in an effort to appeal to a younger generation. Inspired by founder Huang Shi-jie's love of Parisian Left Bank café culture, it infuses tea flavours into French pastries: try a millefeuille oolong. *29th floor, Lane 270, Dunhua South Road, sec 1, T 8772 6160, www.zenique.net*

PROT

Lin Yu-cheng launched PROT (Permanent Revolution of Tea) in 2009, and there are now half a dozen concession counters in department stores, including Shin Kong Mitsukoshi (T 2388 5552), Citylink (T 2748 7728) and Eslite (see p061). More than 20 flavours of either hot or iced pre-brewed bottled teas are on offer. Try the naturally sweet Wenshan Baozhong, flavoured with osmanthus blossoms and poured from a pot of purple clay sourced from Lake Tai in China's Jiangsu province. If you prefer to brew your own or are looking for a stylish gift, the takeaway varieties are packaged in sleek black and pastel-hued casings (above). The most traditional is the lightly roasted and honeyed Dong Ding Oolong, and Taiwan Black Tea, which gives off fragrant notes of orange and lychee. *www.prot.com.tw*

Sunset

Leslie Sun (see p054) set up her concept store in 2015. The range of homewares, design objects and furniture pieces is refined, well-made and regularly witty; the 'Fat Knit' hammock by BLESS is case in point. A Dieter Rams' '606 Universal Shelving System' displays items such as Fort Standard marble candleholders and Paul Loebach copper watering cans. *157, Lane 417, Guangfu South Road*

MeSH

Since becoming part of Taipei's fashion scene in the mid-1990s, Stephane Dou and Changlee Yugin have focused on hip, smart casualwear. Holding shows in car parks and other outré locations has helped the pair build a loyal following. It's apt, then, that their MeSH boutique, opened in 2007, is situated in an alley, somewhat removed from Daan Road's upscale shopping belt. The duo make clothes for men and women, including a selection of highly wearable waffle-knit wool sweaters, gently tailored trousers, oversized cardigans and box-cut tops, as well as some bolder pieces. The minimal white interior features an angular central display bench and a stainless-steel ceiling perforated with laser-cut holes.

3, Lane 116, Daan Road, sec 1, T 8772 8660, www.stephanedou.com

Shiatzy Chen

Since founding her brand in 1978, Wang Chen Tsai-hsia's take on contemporary Eastern chic has drawn the attention of a smart clientele, from politicians and CEOs to celebrities and socialites. The complete range for men and women is on sale at this three-storey flagship store, opened in 2003, where you can expect to see knot buckles, flattened qipao collars and plenty of silk, beading and embroidery, as well as some fine lambswool and cashmere items, all displayed exquisitely throughout the elegant, dark-toned interior. Shoes and handbags, featuring silver and jade ornamentation, also form part of the collection, as does a homewares line; we particuarly liked the linen.
49-1 Zhongshan North Road, sec 2,
T 2542 5506, www.shiatzychen.com

ESCAPES

WHERE TO GO IF YOU WANT TO LEAVE TOWN

When you have the chance to get out of Taipei, head towards the mountains or the sea. The southern half of Taiwan is tropical, and its eastern edge features more than 300km of dramatic coastline, where steep hillsides crash down to rocky shorelines and the odd stretch of sand. The best beaches are at the island's southernmost point near the town of Kenting. Take the High Speed Rail (bullet train) to Zuoying Station, and then transfer to a bus for the final two hours of the trip. You'll be more than ready to check in to the Caesar Park Hotel (6 Kenting Road, Hengchun Township, T 08 886 1888), a well-kept luxury resort near the popular bay at Xiaowan.

Hualien, the largest city on Taiwan's east coast, is three hours from Taipei by train and offers access to the jaw-dropping Taroko Gorge. Available for private rental, Shamo Fengqing house (117-1 Shitiwan, Fengbin Township, T 09 1127 4335) sits on a narrow bluff overlooking the Pacific, and is well worth the one-hour drive.

Capped by the 4,000m Jade Mountain, the highest peak in East Asia discounting the Himalayas, Taiwan's alpine landscape is best appreciated from the Alishan National Scenic Area, where you can hike among 2,000-year-old cedar trees. Jump on the bullet train to Jiayi, from where it's a two-hour bus ride (morning departures only) up into the range. Alishan House (16 West Alishan, Alishan Township, T 05 267 9811) is a comfortable villa set in the forest. *For full addresses, see Resources.*

Onsen Papawaqa, Miaoli

Taiwan is densely populated, but its most impressive mountain range offers plenty of breathing room. There are numerous hot-spring resorts to choose from, though Onsen Papawaqa, which is nestled on a creek bed in a lush valley about two hours' drive south of Taipei, is, architecturally, one of the most compelling. Tang Huang Jeng Design and Associates combined minimalist decor with modern comforts.

The 66 rooms feature rich, local cedar and striking beds set within a raised wooden platform; our choice is the Papawaqa Suite, for its private garden. The raw-concrete and wood exterior, which is gradually being carpeted by moss on one side, overlooks a tranquil pool. A beautiful outdoor spa is another highlight of the property.
58 Yuandun, Jinshui Village, T 03 794 1777, www.papawaqa.com.tw

Xiangshan Visitor Center, Nantou
This 2011 build by Norihiko Dan, which houses a visitor centre, café and offices, sits unobtrusively on the western bank of Sun Moon Lake, Taiwan's largest body of fresh water. Two enormous concrete arches, each of which span 35m, frame knockout views of the lake, and in the other direction, the wooded mountains. A gently inclining green roof provides access to terrace spaces and more vistas.

We suggest checking in to The Lalu hotel (T 04 9285 5311), set in the former holiday home of Chiang Kai-shek. The 98 rooms and suites are designed by architect Kerry Hill, and feature Chinese cypress, marble and terrazzo. The elegant establishment effuses a sense of calm. To get here, it's a three-hour drive south from the capital.
599 Jhongshan Road, Yuchi Township,
T 04 9285 5668, www.sunmoonlake.gov.tw

Taichung City

There are many architectural gems to be found in Taichung City, a three-hour drive from Taipei. The Light of Christ's Salvation Church (428 Jinhua Road; opposite and above) by Taiwanese firm Ambi is defined by the architects as a 'spiritual 7/11' – this does serve to capture their vision for an urban religious sanctuary and community space, although its aesthetics are on an altogether higher plane. Clad in titanium zinc, the church sits offset on a concrete substructure, and voids in the hulking facade allow light in to the calm interiors. Elsewhere in the city, IM Pei and Chen Chi-kwan's tent-like 1960 Luce Memorial Chapel (181 Taichung Port Road) is clad in gold ceramic tiles; and Toyo Ito's National Taichung Theater (101 Huilai Road) is a fluid, cavernous building, with myriad performance spaces and a roof garden.

Lanyang Museum, Yilan
Kris Yao's 2010 Lanyang Museum, which
celebrates the culture and ecosystems
of Yilan County, is a one-hour drive from
Taipei. Yao was inspired by the nearby
wetlands, where upturned slabs of rock
are a distinctive geological feature. A
tilted pyramid clad with aluminium and
glass references their colour and form.
*750 Qingyun Street, sec 3, Toucheng
Township, T 03 977 9700*

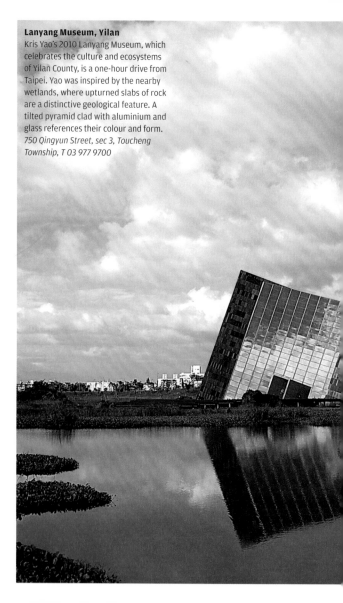

NOTES

SKETCHES AND MEMOS

RESOURCES
CITY GUIDE DIRECTORY

HOTELS
ADDRESSES AND ROOM RATES

Alishan House 096
Room rates:
prices on request
16 West Alishan
Alishan Township
Chiayi County
T 05 267 9811
www.alishanhouse.com.tw

Amba 022
Room rates:
double, from TWD3,100;
Corner Room, from TWD3,600;
Balcony Room, from TWD4,100;
Large Room, from TWD4,700
57-1 Zhongshan North Road, sec 2
T 2525 2828
77 Wuchang Street, sec 2
T 2375 5111
www.amba-hotels.com

Caesar Park Hotel 096
Room rates:
double, from TWD13,200
6 Kenting Road
Hengchun Township
T 08 886 1888
www.caesarpark.com.tw

Éclat 016
Room rates:
double, from TWD13,200
370 Dunhua South Road, sec 1
T 2784 8888
www.eclathotels.com

Eslite Hotel 018
Room rates:
double, from TWD20,500;
Library Suite, from TWD161,400
98 Yanchang Road
T 6626 2888
www.eslitehotel.com

The Grand Hotel 016
Room rates:
double, from TWD9,000
1 Zhongshan North Road, sec 4
T 2886 8888
www.grand-hotel.org

Grand Hyatt 016
Room rates:
double, from TWD11,200
2 Songshou Road
T 2720 1234
www.grand.hyatt.com

Home Hotel Daan 016
Room rates:
double, from TWD12,500
219-2 Fuxing South Road, sec 2
T 8773 8822
www.homehotel.com.tw

Humble House 021
Room rates:
double, from TWD13,800;
Grand Premier Room, TWD21,900
18 Songgao Road
T 6631 8000
www.humblehousehotels.com

Lalu 098
Room rates:
prices on request
142 Zhongxing Road
Yuchi Township
Nantou County
T 04 9285 5311
www.thelalu.com.tw

Mandarin Oriental 016
  Room rates:
  double, from TWD19,000
  158 Dunhua North Road
  T 2715 6888
  www.mandarinoriental.com
Le Méridien 020
  Room rates:
  double, from TWD26,100;
  Executive Suite, from TWD26,100
  38 Songren Road
  T 6622 8000
  www.lemeridien-taipei.com
Onsen Papawaqa 097
  Room rates:
  double, from TWD7,500;
  Papawaqa Suite, TWD12,000
  58 Yuandun
  Jinshui Village
  Taian Township
  Miaoli County
  T 03 794 1777
  www.papawaqa.com.tw
Palais de Chine 016
  Room rates:
  double, TWD11,000
  3 Chengde Road, sec 1
  T 2181 9999
  www.palaisdechinehotel.com
Hotel Proverbs 016
  Room rates:
  double, from TWD17,300
  56 Daan Road, sec 1
  T 2711 1118
  www.hotel-proverbs.com

Regent Taipei 017
  Room rates:
  double, from TWD7,200;
  Tai Pan Suite, from TWD28,900;
  Presidential Suite, TWD180,000
  41 Zhongshan North Road, sec 2
  T 2523 8000
  www.regenttaipei.com
Shamo Fengquing 096
  Room rates:
  double, from TWD2,900
  117-1 Shitiwan
  Fengbin Township
  Hualien County
  T 09 1127 4335
Villa 32 025
  Room rates:
  prices on request
  32 Zhongshan Road
  Beitou
  T 6611 8888
W 016
  Room rates:
  double, from TWD12,400
  10 Zhongxiao East Road, sec 5
  T 8786 5168
  www.starwoodhotels.com

WALLPAPER* CITY GUIDES

Executive Editor
Jeremy Case

Authors
Yoko Choy Wai-ching
Kerstin Yuhua Hsu

Art Editor
Eriko Shimazaki

Photography Editor
Elisa Merlo
**Assistant Photography
Editor**
Nabil Butt

Sub-Editor
Belle Place

Editorial Assistant
Emilee Jane Tombs

Contributors
David Frazier
Rebecca Morris

Interns
Joella Qingyi Kiu
Chloe Lin
Summer Wang

Production Controller
Sophie Kullmann

Wallpaper*® is a
registered trademark
of Time Inc (UK)

First published 2011
Revised and updated
Second edition 2015

© Phaidon Press Limited

All prices and venue
information are correct at
time of going to press,
but are subject to change.

Original Design
Loran Stosskopf
Map Illustrator
Russell Bell

Contacts
wcg@phaidon.com
@wallpaperguides

More City Guides
www.phaidon.com/travel

Phaidon Press Limited
Regent's Wharf
All Saints Street
London N1 9PA

Phaidon Press Inc
65 Bleecker Street
New York, NY 10012

Phaidon® is a registered
trademark of Phaidon
Press Limited

www.phaidon.com

A CIP Catalogue record for
this book is available from
the British Library.

Printed in China

ISBN 978 0 7148 7134 9

PHOTOGRAPHERS

Anew Chen
Xiangshan Visitor Center,
pp098-099

Jeffrey Cheng
Shih Chien University
Gymnasium and Library,
p079

Marc Gerritsen
Hung Kuo Building, p012
Taipei 101, p013
Chiang Kai-shek Memorial
Hall, pp014-015
Regent Taipei, p017
Space Yoga, p025
Huashan 1914 Creative
Park, pp026-027
Mitsui Cuisine, p037
Non Zero, p046
Taipei Fine Arts
Museum, p060
Ri Xing Type Foundry,
pp070-071
MeSH, p094
Shiatzy Chen, p095

Bobby Ho
Taipei city view, inside
front cover
Taipei New Horizon,
pp010-011
Eslite Hotel, pp018-019
Le Méridien, p020
Amba, p022, p023
Cloud Gate Theater,
pp028-029
Boven, p030
Mountain and Sea
House, p031
Raw, p033
Shoun RyuGin, pp034-035
AGCT Apartment, p036
Host Shabu, pp038-039
Café Showroom, p040
Wistaria Tea House, p041
Tua, pp044-045
Mume, p047
Kiosk, p048, p049
Chuo Yin Shi, p052
R&D Cocktail Lab, p053
Leslie Sun, p055
MOCA, p057
Rüskasa, pp058-059
Eslite Gallery, p061
World Trade Center
Square, pp064-065
Koichiro Miura mural,
pp066-067

Galerie Grand Siècle, p069
Zhonghe Sports Center,
p073
Water Moon Dharma
Center, p074, p075
College of Social Sciences,
NTU, pp076-077
Invincible, pp082-083
Club Designer, p084
Everyday Ware & Co, p085,
pp086-087
Artifacts, p088
Ne Sense, p089

Chang-fu Huang
Lanyang Museum,
pp102-103

Sean Marc Lee
Sunset, pp092-093

Ben Murphy
Shi-Yang, pp050-051

Peartree Digital
PROT, p091

TAIPEI
A COLOUR-CODED GUIDE TO THE CITY'S HOT 'HOODS

NORTH TAIPEI
Explore the hot-spring region of Beitou and Taipei's biggest night market in Shilin

CENTRAL TAIPEI
Domineering monuments and Zhongshan North Road characterise the city's core

XINYI
This glassy zone is a hub of shopping malls and skyscrapers housing bars and clubs

UNIVERSITY DISTRICT
Come here for the bohemian vibe, and to sample quality cuisine and upmarket tea houses

EAST DISTRICT
Hipsters frequent the restaurants, bars and boutiques of this fashionable part of town

WANHUA
The city was founded here centuries ago. Visit Longshan Temple and hyperactive Ximen

For a full description of each neighbourhood, see the Introduction.
Featured venues are colour-coded, according to the district in which they are located.